Opera Music

Published by Creative Education
P.O. Box 227
Mankato, Minnesota 56002
Creative Education is an imprint of The Creative Company.

DESIGN AND PRODUCTION BY **ZENO DESIGN**

PHOTOGRAPHS BY Corbis (James L. Amos; Archivo Iconografico, S.A.;
Bettmann; Courtesy of Clyndebourne Festival Opera, Ira Nowinski;
Hulton-Deutsch Collection; Robbie Jack; Adam Woolfitt), Getty Images
(After Louis LE Coeur; Matteo Bazzi/AFP; Timothy A. Clary/AFP; Patrick
Riviere; Beatriz Schiller//Time Life Pictures)

LIBRARY OF CONGRESS CATALOGING-IN-PUBLICATION DATA

Riggs, Kate.
Opera music / by Kate Riggs.
p. cm. — (World of music)
Includes index.
ISBN 978-1-58341-568-9
1. Opera—Juvenile literature. I. Title.

ML1700.R55 2008
782.1—dc22   2006102985

First edition

9 8 7 6 5 4 3 2 1

Opera

MUSIC

KATE RIGGS

CREATIVE EDUCATION

Opera music is an old kind of music. It started more than 300 years ago. It is music that is used with a play. People sing the music. They act out their parts. They do not talk much.

Opera started in a country called Italy (IT-ah-lee).

Some operas have fireworks

The first operas had too much talking. They did not have much singing. So people made operas longer. They made the singers perform their parts, too.

Many operas are stories about people who fall in love.

Operas can be dark and scary

Then people in lots of places started liking opera. They liked to listen to the singers. And they liked to watch them act. A man named Mozart (*MOAT-zart*) wrote lots of opera music. He wrote funny music. He wrote sad music, too. Lots of people liked his music.

Mozart wrote music all the time

Opera singers do not make music by themselves. They need instruments to help them. People in a group play the instruments. The group is called an orchestra (*OR-keh-struh*).

The orchestra sits below the stage

A man named Puccini (*poo-CHEE-nee*) liked writing opera music for big orchestras to play. His music helped people understand the story. The music told them when someone was sad. It told them when someone was happy, too.

A long song for one opera singer is called an aria (AH-ree-ah).

Puccini wrote famous operas

Lots of people liked to go to the opera. They liked to get dressed up for it. They liked to listen to the good music. They liked to have fun with their friends.

Opera singers are actors, too. They dress up in costumes that fit their parts.

People sit close together at the opera

People still like to go to the opera. They like to hear the great singers. They like to see what they look like in person. Lots of people like a singer named Placido Domingo (*PLAH-si-do do-MENG-go*). They like his clear, strong voice.

Only rich people used to go to the opera. Now many people can go.

Opera singer Placido Domingo

People go to an opera house to see an opera. It is a big building. There is a big stage where the singers stand. There are many seats for people to sit in.

Porgy and Bess *is a famous opera from the United States.*

Opera houses are grand places

Some people like to play or sing opera music. Other people like to see the stories acted out. An opera is a fun way to tell a story. Anyone who likes music and stories can have fun watching an opera!

Some opera costumes look scary

GLOSSARY

instruments things people play to make music

opera house a building where people go to see operas

perform to act onstage for other people to watch

play a make-believe show in which a person acts like someone else

An opera singer acts her part

INDEX